Grassroots
leadership

(5)

compiled by

Michael Hall

ISLAND (76) PAMPHLETS

Published December 2005 by Island Publications
132 Serpentine Road, Newtownabbey, Co Antrim BT36 7JQ
© Michael Hall 2005
mikeohall@hotmail.com
http://cain.ulst.ac.uk/islandpublications/

ISBN 1 899510 68 0

Farset Community Think Tanks Project is funded by:

The EU Special Support Programme for Peace and Reconciliation
administered through the **Northern Ireland Community Relations Council**

Printed by Regency Press, Belfast

Introduction

In Pamphlet No. 63 (*At a new crossroads? An overview of community anxieties*), a veteran community activist remarked that those involved in innovative grassroots activities for the past three decades had never really shared their experiences with a wider audience, especially with the new generation of young people now coming into community work. Accordingly, I conducted a series of interviews with a handful of well-known activists, encouraging them to recount their experiences and reflect on the lessons learned – both positive and negative.

All the interviewees were initially reluctant to reminisce about their experiences, concerned that such personal accounts might read as self-promotion. I endeavoured to assure them of the wider benefit in doing so. Some reminded me that personal accounts were inevitably highly subjective, and that others might have different recollections of the same periods in our history. Nevertheless, despite such anxieties, they all agreed to be interviewed.

These interviews were published in Pamphlets 70, 71 and 72. The feedback from community groups was extremely positive and I was prevailed upon to continue with this approach. Further interviews were therefore conducted for pamphlets 75 and 76.

For this particular pamphlet my interviewees are two individuals who have worked tirelessly for the well-being of both our communities: well-known Shankill Road community worker **Louis West**, and **Anne Gallagher** of the 'Seeds of Hope' project.

Michael Hall *Farset Community Thinks Project*

Louis West

I was born at 3 McIvor's Place, Brown Square, at the bottom of Peter's Hill (the town end of the Shankill Road). I had three brothers – George, John and William – and a sister, Elizabeth. The area was staunchly 'Prod' and was located right on what we would term a religious 'interface', so we had our usual skirmishes with our Catholic neighbours. I remember every July we used to erect an Orange arch across the width of Wilson Street, supported by ropes attached to the nearest chimneys. And during the celebrations people had a bit of a dance in both Wilson Street and Brown Street, after which 'The Queen' was played and then everyone went home to bed. Well, on one occasion some Catholics tried to pull down the arch by throwing what looked like a small anchor over the middle of it. But when they all pulled on this contraption not only did the arch come down, but parts of the chimneys also! Two of the Catholics were badly hurt and local people had to get an ambulance to take them to hospital.

Outsiders often assume that all contacts across the interface were antagonistic. Yet many people had good friends on the 'other' side. The Catholic neighbour right behind me was a staunch Republican, and one night he was totally drunk and kept singing 'The Soldier's Song' at the top of his voice. I just couldn't get him to shut up, so in annoyance I threw one of my boots over his rear fence. The next day, of course, I had to go round and wake him up – so that he could retrieve my boot and I could get to work! He and I were good mates.

I am an ex-serviceman. I did a tour of duty in Cyprus under the UN – in 1964, I think it was. After that I was posted to Germany. I still have vivid memories of my time in Cyprus – wee incidents that occurred. Some are light-hearted. I remember there was a donkey lying in the field near where we were stationed at Larnaca; it had just been shot – the bullet had gone right through its neck. And the first-aid man who was with us lifted two bits of tar from the road and blocked the two holes made by the bullet – and the donkey survived! That donkey became our mascot, and whenever our tour of duty was over we had a parade during which we handed over the donkey to the regiment replacing us – who happened to be the Irish Regiment.

And it was strange, when I came home [from doing a tour of duty in Cyprus under the UN], to find myself in a matter of years stuck in the same bloody situation – with riots and troubles and bombs on your own doorstep.

But other memories are sad ones. One time we lost a major and his driver;

their Landrover just disappeared, and was never found. And when you were out on patrol around Larnaca, in the Greek part of the island, you might walk into a wee woman sitting crying. You'd get an interpreter to ask her what was wrong, and she'd tell you that her daughter had been taken away, or her son had been taken away – by the 'other' side in the conflict. As far as I know, there are people in Cyprus who are still trying to locate the bodies of their loved ones, in order to give them a proper funeral.

And it was strange, when I came home, to find myself in a matter of years stuck in the same bloody situation – with riots and troubles and bombs on your own doorstep. By that time I was happily married. At first my wife, Gloria, and I lived in McIvor's Place, but when our first child was expected we moved to the Woodvale. We had two sons – William and Stephen. (Today I also have a daughter-in-law, Geraldine, and a grandson, William Daniel.)

And on 'Bloody Friday', the day the IRA set off 22 bombs across Belfast, in the Sirocco Works we could actually feel the vibration of the bombs going off in Oxford Street bus station – and it was horrible.

My first job when I got out of the Army was in the Sirocco works. They used to take you over from the main works to this yard in Short Strand to do a bit of welding. But it came to the point that because of the Troubles you couldn't have walked, you had to travel by minibus. And on 'Bloody Friday', the day the IRA set off 22 bombs across Belfast, in the Sirocco Works we could actually feel the vibration of the bombs going off in Oxford Street bus station – and it was horrible. Eventually the Sirocco works began to lose orders, and I was made redundant.

When the Troubles began to escalate, the whole vigilante thing spread. The primary momentum behind that was to protect your home; every night we were out standing on the streets until all hours of the morning. There was a lot of fear around, old people especially couldn't get to sleep for night after night. People like myself, Ralf Hazel, Jack Harris, Tommy Aiken and Jackie Hewitt became vigilantes. We might have been seen by some as paramilitaries, but we weren't. I refused to take the oath of allegiance which the paramilitaries demanded, because I told them I had already taken one oath of allegiance – and that was to the British Army – and I wasn't taking any more. But, having said that, if my family had been in any danger and the paramilitaries had a gun they could lend me to protect them with, I would have taken it.

I recall we were doing vigilante duty one night when this guy came over and began to act quite obnoxious. He was drunk and strutting around saying he was in the UVF and trying to tell us what to do. When I began to argue with him he suddenly pulled out a gun. I grabbed it off him and told him to piss off. Which he did: he stumbled up the street and went into a chippie. Now, what I didn't know was that he had his mates already there and he told them that a 'Fenian' had attacked him and taken his gun. So down these boys came and proceeded to viciously attack me. I managed to drop the gun down a drain before they could grab it – for I knew rightly they would use it on me if they got the hold of it. The kicking they were giving me was clearly intended to kill me anyway, and they probably would have succeeded only the other vigilantes finally convinced them that I was a local Protestant.

Some months later I happened to be on a bus and this character gets on and goes upstairs – this was one of the old 'double-deckers'. I got up from my seat and followed him up, and waited. To my satisfaction, the other upstairs passengers eventually left, leaving me alone with him. So I grabbed him and proceeded to beat the shit out of him! I can still remember what I was saying to him as I hit him: 'You were going to leave my wife a widow, you bastard! You were going to leave my kids fatherless!'

I left him there bleeding and got off the bus – and it was obvious that nobody downstairs had realised what had been happening. And then for the next few weeks I sweated, I really sweated! I opened every newspaper expecting to see the headlines: 'Man beaten on bus dies.' And then one day as I was walking along the Shankill here didn't I see him coming along the road towards me. As soon as he saw me he quickly crossed over to the other side. But, ironically, by that stage I just wanted to shake his hand and say: 'Thank God you're alive!'

But it was a real lesson to me. People in this country are too quick to settle things by violence. And I could have gone that way too. Before the Troubles I was one of the local street-fighters, with the nickname 'Joe', after American heavyweight champion Joe Louis. But I am glad I never went down that path. And I was certainly extremely relieved that I hadn't killed yer man. In many ways, even though there were a lot of people very, very angry about what the IRA was doing to their communities, and wanted to retaliate, community work provided a non-violent outlet for some people's energies. I truly believe that community work stopped some people taking up the gun – it was a far better alternative.

> *In many ways, even though there were a lot of people very, very angry about what the IRA was doing to their communities, and wanted to retaliate, community work provided a non-violent outlet for some people's energies.*

Anyway, eventually some of us realised that our communities needed something more constructive, and in particular we needed to be doing something for the young people, as much to keep them occupied and turn their minds away from the constant rioting. So myself, Ralf Hazel, Jack Harris, Tommy Aiken, Robbie Grub and a few others started meeting in Jackie Hewitt's house, trying to come up with ideas. We decided that we would try and open a community centre. But how to raise funds for that? We decided that we could do a collection and put a leaflet round the doors, for ten weeks, and everybody was allocated an area to do this collection. But just to give you some indication of the fear that was about then.... We had decided that pensioners would only be asked to contribute 10p a week, but they often said: 'Here's a pound, that will mean you won't have to come back to me.' You see, at that time people closed their doors at 5 o'clock and they didn't want to open them again. If anybody came rapping the door they just didn't want to know. And to add to the sense of terror there was one bloody eedjit of a paramilitary – I won't give his name – who used to run down the street shooting up into the air – just to keep people awake when they were trying to get asleep! I tripped him up one night – but we'll not go into that!

Anyway, we continued our efforts to get a community centre going. We went from pillar to post without any success. I remember when we met with Community Services, we were dealing with a man who was a real 'phobber-off', and at one meeting I lost the head with him and said: 'Look, we don't want to talk to you no more, you're doing no good to us.' So he was changed and a wee woman called Ruby Ferguson started to deal with us, and she had a far better understanding of how the Troubles were impacting on communities. She eventually got an OBE or something, and she deserved it, and she's the one at the end of the day came to the fore with the funding. We were helped too because at that time Lord Melchett, for the government, was prepared to put a lot of money into setting up community centres.

At that time people closed their doors at 5 o'clock and they didn't want to open them again. If anybody came rapping the door they just didn't want to know.

So Ainsworth Community Centre was established. One of the pensioners, a Mrs Jess, became the first chairperson. And there's a lot of history to Ainsworth. I sometimes get annoyed when people forget just how much work was done through Ainsworth – for children and young people, pensioners, cross-community and all.

Somebody I would like to mention here is Ian Fraser, who was from the Woodvale, and was our contact with NICH [Northern Ireland Children's Holidays]. I remember going up with him to a club on the Whiterock; it was a Sunday so there was booze and a bit of a cabaret on, and you had to buy a ballot ticket as you went in. Anyhow, big Ian won the ballet – £30 – and the compere said 'You can't fucking beat them Shankill Road men'! And this was in the middle of the Whiterock! We were kind of anxious leaving there after that, but nothing happened. Ian was someone who did an awful lot of good work.

The reason we had contact with the Whiterock was a children's holiday scheme. We took fifteen kids from their area away on holidays with fifteen kids from the Woodvale... from Ainsworth. I've already related a few anecdotes about some of my experiences with children's holiday schemes[1], and I know

---

1 See Island Pamphlet No.59 *Home and Away: Some reminiscences on community-based children's holiday projects.*

that Jackie Hewitt has talked[2] about one incident when the father of two of the kids was shot dead by the IRA while we had them on holiday in Stokestown down South, and Jackie had to drive them back to Belfast. I was really very angry about that killing, as was the priest who hosted us in Stokestown.

To make matters worse, we were left down there in British Army tents! We had borrowed them from the Army, and we knew we weren't supposed to take them out of the country, but they were all we had so we didn't tell them where we were going. Anyway, some local IRA men came over to look at them, and the priest had to intervene and explain why they were there. But, to finish the story, we decided just to break the camp up, but because the minibus had gone up to Belfast with the two girls, we were left without transport. I managed to get the hold of Mick Nelson, one of the Dublin busmen[3], and he immediately provided a bus. And that was the first, and perhaps the only time, a Dublin bus has ever come up the Shankill Road! It came up the Shankill at 2 o'clock in the morning to drop each of the kids back to their homes.

When you're dealing with kids, you're not just dealing with them in sport or anything else, you have to tune into their feelings, for a lot of them were troubled, and they were all worried about their mothers and their brothers and whatever – it was just a time when everybody worried about everybody else. In them days the police community relations people and the Army worked alongside us. I remember we were invited over to Hollywood Barracks for sports events, and we also got the young people playing dominos, or darts, or pool – that sort of thing. It was active, it was competitive, and kids need things to be competitive about, and I loved those days.

You had to be very inventive and adaptable when trying to help young people. I remember teaching a wee lad to play darts – just so that he would learn how to count. There was another lad who I coaxed to join the Army – his mother had died and he was always getting into trouble – and he had just too much energy. I convinced him to join the Army, but I'd overlooked the fact that he had 'UVF' tattooed on his

And that was the first, and perhaps the only time, a Dublin bus has ever come up the Shankill Road! It came up the Shankill at 2 o'clock in the morning to drop each of the kids back to their homes.

arm. We got him to go and sign all the necessary papers, only for him to be turned down when they saw the tattoo. I ended up giving him the money to get it tattooed over. Then I enlisted the help of the police community relations people in Tennent Street RUC station and we managed to set up another interview for him, and this time he got into the Army and did his nine years there. He turned out a nice lad.

---

2 See Island Pamphlet No.72 *Grassroots leadership (3): Recollections by Jackie Hewitt and Jim McCorry.*

3 In the wake of a Loyalist bomb in Dublin some busmen in Rahenny decided to form a North-South friendship group, and over the years provided regular support to the work of Louis West and his colleagues.

I used to go and talk all the time on behalf of young people brought up before the courts. It came to the point where even the judges knew your name. Judge McGiver used to say, 'Is it yourself, Mr West; what can we do for you today?' That was just one of your roles.

Some of my other court 'appearances' were somewhat amusing. Just after Internment I was asked to go down and give a reference for a man from the Shankill who had been lifted by the police. And I got up and spoke about this particular man. He used to do house repairs, and I said: 'I know this gentleman well, and any time there's a pensioner needs a slate put on their roof he does it...' I went on about him being a good family man with a business to run. Anyway, after I'd finished, the judge turned around to me and said: 'Mr West, you've stood there for the last half an hour and you've done nothing but commit perjury. Is it not a fact that when this gentleman was interned there was a huge sigh of relief went through the Woodvale?' And I couldn't do anything else but laugh, because it was true! The man was eventually released, but he changed after that, because Internment did scare the crap out of some of them.

We then started inviting pensioners from Divis and Springfield Road over to Ainsworth, pensioners even came up from Dublin, and they always had a lovely day.

The first management committee at Ainsworth comprised Jackie Hewitt, Tommy Aiken, Jackie Donnal, Robbie Grub, Jack Harris, Ralf Hazel, Betty McMillan and myself – and Lorraine Aston who came later on.

As well as working to improve the wellbeing of the local community, we also tried to provide entertainment for people, because in those days you couldn't travel too far outside your own area for such things. Ainsworth brought some great entertainment into the Woodvale. I booked the likes of Roly Daniels, George Hamilton IV, Frankie McBride and the Polka Dots, and a lot of other good groups and entertainers. And that's what the Shankill Road needed, because those were depressing times.

We used Ainsworth for different activities to keep kids out of trouble. We had a boxing club and two snooker tables. We also had a pre-school playgroup. We had our pensioners group who went down in Dublin; this is where the contact between the Dublin busmen and Ainsworth came to the fore, through Tommy Dickson, the 'Duke'.[4] We then started inviting pensioners from Divis Flats and Springfield Road over to Ainsworth, pensioners even came up from Dublin, and they always had a lovely day: they enjoyed their singing, they enjoyed their wee dance and their wee game of bingo, it was their day. Consequently then we got invited down to Dublin, and again the Dublin busmen made all this happen. And we had some laughs... I remember we took a crowd of pensioners

---

4 Former footballer Tommy Dickson was known as the 'Duke of Windsor' because he once skippered Linfield Football Club whose home ground was Windsor Park, Belfast.

into the Lord Mayor's parlour in Dublin, and as you go in there's a big pendulum clock, and on it are two large letters: 'S' and 'F'. And this pensioner from the Woodvale walks over to it and says, 'Them Sinn Féinners get in every fucking where!' We just took a fit of laughing, and then explained to her that the letters stood for 'Slow' and 'Fast'. And some of them were saying that they didn't know St Patrick had knights, because there's a room there with St. Patrick's Knights on it. It was all very educational.

But that was one of the things that sustained us all even when the Troubles were at their worst. The fact that, even with the paramilitaries prepared to bomb and shot each other, there were still people that just wanted to sit down together and enjoy life. Now, the ones from the Woodvale still wanted to be under the Crown. They were happy to sit down and take drinks with Catholics, but that didn't mean that they were giving up their British heritage. And the same thing with the people from the South – when they came up here, they weren't feeling any less Irish, you know. We just got on and enjoyed one another's company, as human beings.

Tommy Dickson and I went down to Dublin quite a lot, courtesy of the Dublin busmen. At one time we were meeting Taoiseach Bertie Ahern quite regularly. But there was one occasion when Tommy and I were invited down to meet President Mary Robinson. And I remember when we got off the train some of the Dublin busmen were standing waiting for us, and they wouldn't let us go to the pub across the road from the station for a pint – they knew our form only too well! 'No, no!' they insisted, 'Go down and meet Mary first and then you can get all the drink you want afterwards.' So we got threw into a minibus and we went to Phoenix Park, then to meet Mary Robinson. Mary welcomed us very warmly, gave a lovely speech, and then says: 'There's a wee drop of the black stuff for those who love that type of refreshment.' And I never tasted Guinness like it! Then the whiskey came out....

Community workers were always receiving threats from different sources. I was threatened during the Ulster Workers' Council strike. I was informed that this certain person was going to 'put a bullet' in my head. And I got a hold of that fella and me and him spoke face to face. I then went round to the local paramilitary commander to complain, but he supported him. So I says 'Well, I'm warning you – if he's coming after me with guns I'll protect myself.'

As well as that, there was constant harassment from the paramilitaries. They even robbed Ainsworth, took everything out of it – even the salt-sellers! The paramilitaries also wanted to use Ainsworth to make money. We kept them out

But that was one of the things that sustained us all even when the Troubles were at their worst. The fact that, even with the paramilitaries prepared to bomb and shot each other, there were still people that just wanted to sit down together and enjoy life.

to the extent that we told them if they were caught using the place we would probably lose our grant from the City Council. They wanted to use it every month for selling drink or having a cabaret, because their own club wasn't as big as ours.

I went to see the UDA leadership but was told that each area had to raise money some way. Shortly after that, twenty-four of them walked into Ainsworth when I was there with Jackie Hewitt and Jackie Donnal. And one big fella pointed the finger at me: 'You went over our fucking heads, you need a bullet in *your* fucking head!' I tried to keep my temper, 'cause I'm terrible when I lose my temper. So we sat down and tried to talk to them, and all you got from them was: 'Look, they're using everything they want in the Falls to raise fucking funds and yet you're stopping us here.' I says to them: 'You've your own bloody club over there. Why do you need ours? And, anyway, *who* got you that club, who got you Mayo Street? Who had to negotiate to get it for you? Me!' Anyway, it was important to keep the peace even within our own side, so eventually we agreed that they could have it once every now and then, provided that the money was used for prisoners and their families and not to buy guns. Whether it was or not I never knew.

I had a lot of enemies, I was getting a lot of phone calls... I don't know how my wife stuck it, there were that many threatening phone calls coming into the house. There were ball-bearings put through our front window; there were guns deliberately buried in the garden.

I helped moved people out of the Springfield Road, including the last Prod to be moved from there. I moved one family into a vacant house only to find that the gentleman who owned it was one of the top men in the UDA and I was ordered to remove them, because this man had it earmarked for one of his relatives – otherwise I would get a bullet in the head. So I had a lot of enemies, I was getting a lot of phone calls... I don't know how my wife stuck it, there were that many threatening phone calls coming into the house. There were ball-bearings put through our front window; there were guns deliberately buried in the garden. We were under pressure from all over the place.

It was then that my wife and I split up, and I moved temporarily into the offices of the Woodvale and Shankill Housing Association. But one night I was petrol-bombed out of there – and I had to jump over the flames! I can't prove it, but I could nearly bet that it was local paramilitaries behind it. When I jumped over the flames to escape I was completely naked – I had been asleep at the time – and once out on the street my hands automatically went to cover my private parts. So I'm standing there and this lady came over, and what did she offer me? A pair of slippers to keep my feet warm!

I wasn't the only one under pressure, of course. Jackie Hewitt had his windows put in one time. And there was one area, which was still mixed then and had its own residents' committee. And the understanding – from the paramilitaries – was that if a Protestant left a house then it had to be given to a Protestant, to keep the ratio equal. But the chairman of the residents' committee didn't agree to that, so they booby-trapped his front gate and he lost a leg. That was the type of fear that you had – horrendous fear sometimes. The thing was that every day you just got up and you didn't know what might be coming towards you.

Of course, there were also plenty of light-hearted moments. One time I was asked to chair a meeting in a community centre in East Belfast. Jackie Redpath, myself and Ian Fraser went over. The reason I was asked was because there was a couple of DUP councillors there always trying to hog the limelight, and somebody had to tell them to sit down. And that's what I did with one of them – told him to just sit on his backside and let other people talk. You see, community groups were always wary of politicians bouncing in and using the good work being done at community level to promote themselves. But, anyway, we ended up having to stay all night in that particular community centre because a riot started outside. We couldn't leave the place, there were petrol bombs and everything else being thrown. Redpath, big Ian and myself had to stay there – though they had a pool table and drink, so it wasn't too bad!

Redpath and the Shankill Community Council were fighting the slum clearance. A lot of housing protests took place at that time. For example, whenever the Housing Executive built public housing they expected to get their money back in 60 years, but when Ray Carter, who was the minister of state, came along he decided to increase the rent so they could get their money back in 30 years. So quite an extensive rent protest was launched. Housing was a major concern. Hughie Smyth, Jim Smyth, Jackie Redpath, Hughie Stockman, Freddie Weir, May Robinson and myself... we were all tied up in housing action of one sort or another in them days.

I remember attending cross-community meetings and having to walk home at two in the morning, because I didn't have the taxi fare. And they were rough days, all sorts of things were happening, and it wasn't safe to be walking around at night.

I didn't stick to Ainsworth, I went outside the area to meet with others, to discuss how we could all work for peace. In particular, Ian Fraser had introduced me to Joe Camplisson's community development initiative[5] at 359 Antrim Road. I remember attending cross-community meetings at '359' and having to walk home at two in the morning, because I didn't have enough for the taxi fare. Unless Ian Fraser was there – he would have dropped me home. And they were rough days, all sorts of things were happening, and it wasn't safe to be walking around at night.

But it was amazing the range of people we sometimes had in that room. And

5 See Island Pamphlet No.70 *Grassroots leadership (1): Recollections by May Blood and Joe Camplisson.*

whenever important issues were discussed which we wanted fed back into the different organisations, Ian would have gone back to the UDA, Joe would have went and talked to the Provies, and Jim McCorry would have been involved as well. The people we would have met there included representatives from the IRA, the UDA... the full range of paramilitary organisations.

Bill McCarthy was a teacher in Bolton Street College in Dublin and the dean was Eamon de Burca. They asked me to go down and talk to some of their students about the conflict. Four of us – myself, Betty Rice, Danny Godfrey and Joe Camplisson went down to speak, and Tommy Dickson drove the minibus. I thought we were just going to talk in a wee room, but we ended up in a massive hall, and instead of the dozen students I

But it was amazing the range of people we sometimes had in that room.... The people we would have met there included representatives from the IRA, the UDA... the full range of paramilitary organisations.

had been expecting, there were nearly 300! We each got up and said a few words, then we answered questions. One man said to me, 'Mr West, you come from West Belfast?' I said, 'That's correct.' He says, 'And your local MP is Gerry Adams. What backing do you get from Gerry Adams?' I told him that I was sure he knew full well that if I was caught talking to Gerry Adams there would be that many bullets in me you'd be able to sell me to the scrapyard. I got a handclap for that. Then I added: 'Now that you've asked me that... *you* take a message to Gerry Adams from this platform, that if he can get the IRA to lay down the gun and the bomb then maybe in a few years' time he'll be in the same room as the Rev Ian Paisley.' And I got a standing ovation for that.

I then put Tommy Dickson on the spot, and I told the audience about Tommy having the courage to get the first Catholic to play for Linfield. And when the focus went onto Tommy he says to them: 'You know I thought I was only coming down here to drive the minibus.' Tommy's a cracker!

Former UDA leader Davy Payne was working with handicapped ex-combatants, and it was after seeing his project that myself, Joe Camplisson and Tommy Dickson went down to Dublin to see Johnny Giles – the skipper of the Irish football team – about arranging an all-Ireland football team to play Holland. Derek Dougan got members of the Northern Ireland team to take part, and a man called Ono de Haan sorted out the Dutch team. With the proceeds of the match we were able to buy a minibus for the handicapped project. Harry Chicken helped us with this.

Another time myself, Tommy Dickson and Johnny Giles planned to bring Linfield down South to play Shellburn, until we found out how much it was going to cost to pay for the police. You had to have so many policemen there to ensure there was no trouble, and the game organisers had to pay for each one of them – at £100 each! We couldn't afford that so we had to cancel it. It was a big disappointment, for the Dublin busmen had already sold hundreds of tickets. I dare say you don't have to pay for the police to attend matches these days.

Tommy Dickson has done some marvellous things – along with Joe Camplisson and Jim Boyce, who was the chairman of the IFA [Irish Football Association]. I remember when Northern Ireland was to play Moldova, and Joe, who was actually working in Moldova, managed to bring the two presidents over to watch the match – one was the president of Moldova, the other was from its breakaway region of Transdniestria, and there was a civil war going on between them.[6]

Not that it was all plain sailing. Tommy got up one morning, where he was living in Taughmonagh, and there was this wreath sitting on top of the minibus. And he had to go round to the paramilitaries and ask them what they were playing at. They said it was just some eedjit acting on his own. That is another thing that needs to be stressed. I'm not saying that every paramilitary commander was against us, for some of the attacks originated from lone individuals who just took an notion to do these things. Anyway, Tommy went to see the leader up there and the leader said, 'Look, we know the work you're doing, you just carry on with it, and try to forget about that incident.'

And I have gone up on different times to the bars the paramilitaries would drink in and had a drink and a chat with them. The barriers we broke was immeasurable.

I remember the night that Davy Payne got up and done this speech, and he was talking about when he was in charge of youth training trying to keep the kids away from paramilitaries and everything else. Next thing Davy was shot. The paramilitaries were more or less saying that Davy had disowned them and was preventing them recruiting.

On one occasion I was approached by UDA leader Andy Tyrie for advice. This was during the time when the paramilitaries were making leather goods in the Kesh, and they needed an outlet to sell it; they wanted to open a shop in the Shankill. And I was asked if I knew anywhere where we could make contacts for them, maybe sell these goods in America. So I introduced them to Strokestown, because

I'm not saying that every paramilitary commander was against us, for some of the attacks originated from lone individuals who just took an notion to do these things.

I knew there was a co-op there, run by a priest we had good links with. Two of the Loyalists went down with me for a visit, and we saw where they did basket weaving in a building behind the chapel. And when one of the Loyalists was walking round the place, he whispered to me: 'An aul petrol bomb would go well here.' Absolutely mad!

Once when we were in Wales with a group of children a major incident

6 See Island Pamphlet No.61 *The search for conflict resolution: lessons drawn from a community development strategy.*

occurred back home – I can't remember exactly what it was, a bad bombing or something – and Professor John Borland from Bangor University, and Susan James, a local lady – the two main organisers of that particular project – suggested a joint religious service for all victims. But the leaders from the Catholic side would not allow it to happen until they rang home and asked every one of the parents if they were happy for their child to attend a joint service. John Borland and Susan James couldn't understand it, they hadn't foreseen that there could be a problem over such a thing. I suppose it educated them a bit about the depth of our divisions. But we really appreciated all the work those two put into that holiday scheme, and also the students of Bangor University who raised the money for it.

There was one very sad incident. The IRA had abducted a UDR[7] soldier, and in retaliation the 'Shankill Butchers'[8] had abducted a Catholic man. Now, the Catholic man's daughter worked in the *Irish News*, and I was asked by Jim Fitzpatrick, the newspaper's owner, if I could do anything about finding out who had him, and the chances of getting him released. Myself, Joe Camplisson, John Carson, Jackie Hewitt and others put the word out as much as we could – Joe put it through his community, we put it through ours – to say that we'd be available to arrange a swap.

During the time of the UWC strike we were up every night, we made stew at times when the electric was off; people even slept in the Centre because they'd no heat.

We gave out the phone number of Ainsworth, and asked those involved to ring us and let us know where we could go and pick the two gentlemen up. And we sat for hours in Ainsworth waiting for news. Now, and this makes me really angry, the wee man was found two streets away – the 'Butchers' had cut his throat – and the UDR man was found on a country lane with a bullet in his head.

Jim Fitzpatrick and I became very good friends. He gave me money to buy new clothes the time I was petrol-bombed. He also offered me money if I needed to get out of the country.

Ainsworth Community Centre was used during the EEC meat days.[9] And it was a depot for the community to bring stuff which was to be sent to help people in Eastern Europe, such as the orphanages in Romania, or the victims of the earthquake in Armenia. Then during the time of the Ulster Workers Council strike (1974) we were up every night, we made stew at times when the electric was off; people even slept in the Centre because they'd no heat. It was kind of what you'd have done during the Second World War, and indeed a lot of the older people used to sit down and reminisce about that period. Half of them

---

7 Ulster Defence Regiment, a locally-based British Army regiment formed in 1970.

8 Label given to a particularly notorious gang of Shankill Road Loyalists who not only killed but mutilated their victims.

9 When EEC stocks of meat, butter, cheese, etc., got too high community organisations and churches were allowed to distribute it cheaply.

never slept, they just came into the Centre... the door was more or less always open. And we got the flash lamps and everything else ready.

I've had bad times, but I've also been very lucky with some of the people I've meet, who did not look at anything else only that you were a human being. Not only those who I've already mentioned, but people like Johnny Marmion, Freddie Weir, May Robinson, Annie Morrison, Hughie Stockman, Jim Smith and others. And not only people from Northern Ireland, but from down South. And even England – the likes of Lord Hylton coming over here regularly, showing the interest he did.

When prisoners were getting released, Ainsworth and Farset arranged to employ some of them. The point was to rehabilitate them back into the community. Yet a few came out of prison expecting to get golden gloves put on them. And one of them had been a member of the 'Butchers', and the IRA stated that they would go after every 'Butcher', no matter whether there was peace or not. And I remember a couple of them wanted to put guards on the door of the Centre, but we said 'no way'. But those are some of the problems you had to deal with.

And again, the ACE [Action for Community Employment] scheme was a good means of doing things; we had people out doing gardens and whatever other types of employment we could find for them. I still feel angry that government decided to end the ACE scheme. I thought it was brilliant, it enabled communities to run an awful lot of projects and activities. We had two ACE schemes going in Ainsworth Community Centre.

I recall when UDA leader John McMichael was working on the *Common Sense* document. And that was a good title, because surely if we all showed a wee bit of common sense both communities could find a way of living with each other. At that time too a Professor Darcy was involved in helping the Protestant community. Not only with regards putting together documents, but he set up a training session on media presentation and things like that. You know: when you're sitting in a TV studio there's things that you shouldn't do – like, with your hands and whatever – because it distracts people and they end up missing

> *I still feel angry that government decided to end the ACE scheme. I thought it was brilliant, it enabled communities to run an awful lot of projects and activities.*

the point that you're trying to make. And how to answer properly and see what the other person is trying to say. It was a great education.

As far as I am concerned the war is over, and it's time we got back to normality. And all I can say to certain people is: whatever you were doing during the war, don't be thinking you can get away with it for too long afterwards. Because we need to get back to normality and we need to build up our communities again; we need to get our youth back on the go again, we have to stop them torturing old people. Now, how do we do it? Everybody is coming up with different ideas, and no one person has the answer. But 100 people with all different ideas could surely come up with something which could work.

As for Unionist politicians, once they got voted in they forgot about you. Unionists candidates were either from the Orange Order or were well known to the public – as businessmen or military men, people like that. But most Unionist politicians never did much, nor did they even care much, for working-class Protestants. In fact, there used to an aul saying that the only way for Prods to get anything done was to go and see Gerry Fitt.

During the Second World War, Protestants and Catholics fought together in the British Army against a common enemy. Is that what we still need? Do we need to have a common enemy before Catholics and Protestants can come together again? Well, we have one. The common enemy is poverty, bad housing, no employment for our young people. I worked in Ross's Mill when I was 14, and I had to run down the Falls every night when I finished work at 8 o'clock – sometimes 10 o'clock if you were working overtime, just to get a couple of extra pound. Our common enemy then was poverty, and it's *still* the common enemy. On top of the poverty, our communities have been devastated, by the Troubles and by the planners and the redevelopers. We have lost 27,000 of a population of West Belfast.

Our common enemy then was poverty, and it's still the common enemy. On top of the poverty, our communities have been devastated, by the Troubles and by the planners and the redevelopers.

We cannot afford to go back to the way it was. I remember an old woman who gassed herself because she just couldn't take any more of it. And I remember seeing people walking around with almost dead eyes – you could see from their faces that it was grinding them down. We *cannot* allow things to go back to that ever again. We have got to get away from guns once and for all. When someone has possession of a gun it does something to him, it goes to his head, and he becomes highly dangerous.

These are just some of the incidents in my community 'career'. And maybe they come over a bit of all over the place. But a lot of what happened I've been putting to the back of my mind, trying to forget it now. Sometimes when I think of it I get a lump in my throat, whenever I get hurt or angry. Or other times I get, you know, like a burning desire that I have to do something about it – and have been trying for over 30 years.

We have so many religions and nationalisms in the world you'd think that people just wanted to find reasons to keep the human race divided. And it is hard for people to move forward when hate has taken the place of common sense. Instead of realising that all we need for everyday life is to treat each other with love and understanding. Life's far too short to worry about all those things which attempt to divide us.

Anne Gallagher

I grew up in a really happy, loving family; I had seven brothers and three sisters. I never wanted any other career only nursing, and I still keep in contact with the friends I made when I started nursing in the Fever Hospital. However, it was also the first time that I had experienced anyone dying, because there were many babies who died of gastroenteritis. It was actually on the night Internment was introduced that I watched a little baby – a little boy – dying, and his parents were absolutely devastated. It was the first time I had witnessed so much trauma and so many tears. Up until then I had never thought about babies dying, and it was heartbreaking. I was still upset when, shortly afterwards, Matron sent for me, to inform me that she had just received a phone call from my doctor at home in Bellaghy, to say that my father and three of my brothers had been lifted as part of Internment. I couldn't comprehend what she was telling me, I just couldn't grasp it. I was allowed to go straight home, where I found my mother heavily sedated, and it was all such a shock to me.

And that was the beginning of a whole new life for me and my family. I was the eldest girl, and it was terrible watching the pain my mother and father went through. I later asked my brothers whether they had been involved in the IRA prior to Internment but they said that they hadn't – it was the actual experience of being interned which motivated them, especially Dominic. Dominic was kept in the longest and then when he was released the security forces never really left him alone. In response, along with his friends Francis Hughes and Tom McElwee, who both later died on hunger strike, he formed the local Provisional IRA unit.

My aunt had a pub in Clonard in West Belfast and you'd go there and listen to people telling their stories of terror, and you got this real sense of a community that was really suffering. But I still didn't have any sense of why my brothers were doing what they were doing. Then going straight back to nursing, trying to normalise everything. It was all so confusing for me, and with not really having anybody to talk to or share what I was going through, I suppose I buried it all.

> *I still didn't have any sense of why my brothers were doing what they were doing. It was all so confusing for me, and with not really having anybody to talk to or share what I was going through, I suppose I buried it all.*

And all the time, especially when I worked in the Royal [Victoria Hospital], I was constantly faced with seeing the end result of what the conflict was doing to people. Just to see their wounds, and the amount of care that went into helping people recover, and knowing that somebody had inflicted all this on them, just really devastated me. Many times I'd be choking back the tears, and I was feeling a lot of their pain, because I felt so much love and compassion for people, no matter who they were.

The security forces would raid our house regularly – often acting in a very brutal manner – and it used to break my mother's heart. During these raids the loudest thing I heard – far above the banging on the front door or the sound of the helicopter – would be her praying as they were searching the house: 'Sacred Heart of Jesus, I place all my trust in you!' She still says that prayer, it's like a little mantra for her. And one time I asked a police sergeant: '*Why* do you keep coming to this house?' And he told me that it was no pleasure for him: 'Up in the police station we've great respect for your mother... but this is our job.' And I think that was true; they'd get a phone call from wherever to say 'raid that house' – and that was it, they had to go.

But I was experiencing the conflict from both sides. On one occasion, after having spent a few days at home on leave, during which time the police had yet again raided our house, the next evening I was back in the Royal nursing this policeman in intensive care. He was on life support and my task was to look after him. And he was naked... the whole thing about nakedness is that you've no clothing to identify you, no uniform – at that moment you're just another human being. Everything that was intimate

Those nights could be so long. Through the blinds you could see the ambulances pulling up outside, their sirens wailing, and you'd have all these thoughts going on in your head about the terrible things that were happening around you on a daily basis in Belfast.

I had to do for him, and to me it didn't matter that he was a policeman. But it did seem ironic that only the day before his colleagues had totally controlled our house and now – from when I went on duty at 8pm until I came off the following morning – this policeman's life was totally under *my* control, as I nursed him, washed him, cared for him, talked to him, and wondered what was going on inside his unconscious mind. And I'm thinking: I really care for you, you're just somebody who was on duty and this is what has happened to you.

Those nights could be so long. Through the blinds you could see the ambulances pulling up outside, their sirens wailing, and you'd have all these thoughts going on in your head about the terrible things that were happening around you on a daily basis in Belfast.

And then, after Dominic's face appeared alongside Francis Hughes on an RUC 'most wanted' poster, and he later became leader of the INLA[1], the media began to constantly focus on him. And although I was proud of my background, I was actually glad when I got married that I now had a different surname, because I didn't want to be McGlinchey any more, I didn't want people saying to me: 'Are you anything to yer man?' Because I didn't know what to say to

---

1. Irish National Liberation Army.

19

people. I didn't know how to explain my brothers' involvement in the conflict. For on my days off I'd go for visits to Long Kesh [the Maze prison], or Crumlin Road, and I'd sit and look at my brothers and know just how much I loved them.

You never knew what might be around the corner. During the time they were looking for Dominic, he and Seamus Grew and Roderick Carroll were intending to drive back over the border. At the last minute they were warned that the RUC were waiting to arrest Dominic[2] further up the road. So he got out of the car and it continued over the border where the police riddled it with bullets and the two fellas were shot dead. This was during the 'shoot to kill' period.

So during the week I'd be totally involved in my work as a nurse, then I'd go home at the weekends, and I'd look at mammy's face and wonder what she was feeling as a mother. And during the period when four of my brothers were inside – Dominic, Paul, Sean and Michael (although he was only in a short time) – I'd arrive home and four cardboard boxes – for their food parcels – would be sitting on the kitchen table, with their names on them. And mammy would have made treacle bread and soda bread to put in each box, and she was constantly weighing each box to make sure that it didn't go over the permitted weight for going into Long Kesh. As a mother that was the way she passed her week, making up these boxes and doing other things for her family. Paul spent about 17 years inside, Sean about 18, and Dominic would have done 15 years. It's a long time to have such a large part of your family imprisoned.

Sean had got out of prison ten days before Christmas. He had been given six life sentences for his involvement in the Coleraine bombing[3] but with no release date. However, the Northern Ireland Secretary Tom King asked to see some of the lifers' parents and he met mammy. He was very impressed by her and then he met Sean and out of that Sean got a release date. He was only out when he was briefly lifted by the police who told him that he wouldn't see Christmas. He took the threat seriously, and didn't want mammy to have to go through a funeral at Christmas. So he agreed to go with me to this retreat type of place I knew about just outside Paris until things settled down – it was a lay community with people there from all over the world.

Paul spent about 17 years inside, Sean about 18, and Dominic would have done 15 years. It's a long time to have such a large part of your family imprisoned.

The retreat was located in a beautiful little village. I would have found it impossible to find – after the flight we had to go by the Metro into Paris and then out by train – but Sean had no problem with maps and timetables. When I expressed my surprise at this he started telling me about one of the escapes from Long Kesh and how they had to study maps and the weather. And when he was taken anywhere in a van, even though the windows were blacked out, he had

---

2. In February 1994 Dominic McGlinchey was killed by gunmen near his home in Drogheda.

3. Four women and two men were killed by the car-bomb explosion at Railway Road on 12 June 1973.

been able to develop like an inner sense of which direction he was travelling in. We eventually got to this place and because it was coming up to Christmas it was absolutely full, but we were accommodated in two wooden sheds sitting in the garden, in each of which there was just a small bed and a little locker. I stayed with Sean two days and then returned home. However, a few days later I got a phone call from him to say that, death threat or not, he had decided to come home for Christmas. And shortly afterwards he moved down South.

When I got married I too had moved down South – to Dublin – and whenever Dominic, Sean or Paul were on the run they would have come down to see me. And even though this meant that our phone was tapped and I often found myself followed about by Special Branch, I was always delighted to see my brothers and to be able to cook them a meal. But then they started having meetings in our house – with people I didn't know – and I wasn't happy about that. I decided to visit Sean and tell him that I didn't want them using the house any more, because I didn't know who these people were, or what they were planning, and that deep down I was an absolute passivist and didn't believe in the taking of human life.

I thought that I too was dying, yet I was in a place that I didn't mind being. ... Whether it was a spiritual thing or something I don't know, but I had no fear of dying, for that had been somehow taken away from me.

So I travelled up to Belfast on the train, where Sean picked me up, informing me that we were going to my brother Paul's house near Toome Bridge for a meal. I never got that meal because we were involved in this horrific car crash and I ended up in intensive care in Belfast. When the car crashed, Sean was able to get out of it, but then another vehicle came along, didn't see our car – with me trapped inside – and it was the second collision which caused all my injuries. And when I was in intensive care, and drifting in and out of consciousness, I started getting these flashbacks of when I myself had nursed patients who had been on life support. While I was in intensive care four people in my ward died – I watched the trolley being taken in during the night to wheel them out. I thought that I too was dying, yet I was in a place that I didn't mind being. I went in and out of this kind of.... whether it was a spiritual thing or something I don't know... but I had no fear of dying, for that had somehow been taken away from me.

There was a little woollen doll that hung on the end of the nurses' station. And when I started to recover, the first thing I asked for was this wee doll. Because I'd seven brothers growing up I never remember having a doll. It had been knit by a nurse who worked on another ward so they sent for her and brought her up to intensive care to meet me. She must have thought I'd turned mental, you know, when I relayed to her how much I liked it. She asked me to give her photographs of my three daughters and from these she knit three little woollen 'nurses', resembling each of my children. The reason I'm telling this story is that before my accident I was working with severely mentally-handicapped people, who couldn't tell their own stories in the way others could. And now, I too was paralysed ... I couldn't move a muscle, and I had nurses doing things to me and I couldn't say, 'You didn't dry my hair, you didn't wipe my bottom', and I was aware of the intrusion of that and not being able to verbalise how I felt. So in a way that little doll summed up that experience for me. When I was well enough to return to nursing, I was asked to give a talk to a group of nurses and doctors about being an advocate for people who don't have a voice, just as I had been without a voice for part of my time in intensive care. And I used that doll in my presentation.

When they moved me out of intensive care I was put in the orthopaedic ward. And it was while I was there that I really made the decision that I was going to do something about the 'Troubles'. In the bed beside me was a woman, Margaret, who was from the Shankill. She had been going to work one morning in a taxi under which the IRA had planted a bomb, and when it exploded she sustained severe leg injuries and the driver lost a leg. Then one day a nurse came in and put a curtain around her and they brought in this man in a wheelchair – he was the taxi driver. He hadn't seen Margaret since the day of the bombing and he was going into theatre to have his other leg amputated – but before he did he wanted to meet the woman who had been in the back seat of his taxi. I thought: I can't believe this, that I'm in the next bed listening to this unbelievably tragic human story – and I just couldn't stop crying. I'd love to meet Margaret again, I'd love to know how she is.

In the mornings those with leg injuries were brought down to the gym for exercises, where there were these three red steps, and the big achievement was be to be able to walk up these three steps. There were two young lads there – one Catholic, the other Protestant – and both of them were there as a result of punishment shootings. And one day the physio said to me: 'Anne, it's a pleasure working with you because we rehabilitate you to go back home so that you can get on with your life and try to forget about all this, but we rehabilitate those two young people who will return to their communities and soon afterwards

I knew in my heart and soul that the nurse part of me, the compassion that I had in me, could make a difference, that surely I could do some wee thing to make a difference to all the terrible trauma that I saw around me.

some other young people will come back in their place.' And I thought to myself: 'Yes, you do rehabilitate me, but no, I'm not going to get on with my life and just forget about this.' I knew in my heart and soul that the nurse part of me, the compassion that I had in me, could make a difference, that surely I could do some wee thing to make a difference to all the terrible trauma that I saw around me.

Anyway, as I was still some time rehabilitating when I went back to Dublin, I thought of occupying my time with a bit of writing. At the time I was fascinated by Deirdre Manifold, who had written many books of a social content and put the money she made into social projects. So I asked this journalist friend if she would help me write an article about Deirdre for inclusion in the *RTE Guide*. But she replied: 'What about telling your *own* story?' And I eventually agreed that she would help me do that. I needn't go into the details, but the idea started to get out of hand, and when my friend began to express an eagerness to have 'the book on the shelves by Christmas' I thought to myself: no, no, this isn't about getting a book on the shelves for Christmas! So I backed away from the idea and it never went ahead. However, I am relating this because of its relevance to what would later transform my life.

During the time when the idea of writing a book was still a possibility, someone had said to me: 'Did you ever ask your brothers why they got involved in the IRA, and why they did what they did?' That was the most challenging question anyone could have put to me, because it was something I had always avoided. I obviously couldn't have asked my brothers questions like that during prison visits, but nor did I ever ask them when they were released. Yet such questions always kind of haunted me. In particular, the one question that I did want to get an answer to was why Sean planted the Coleraine bomb.

> *He talked about the deaths and the injuries, especially the little kids who were injured. And you know, he just didn't realise that people would be killed, and deeply regretted that it had ever happened.*

So I decided to travel up from Dublin – by bus, as I still couldn't drive at this stage of my rehabilitation – to see Sean, who was living in Culdaff, County Donegal. He knew I was interested in writing a book, and so he took me for a walk along the beach. And without me saying anything to him, he remarked: 'You do know that if you write a book, you're going to be inundated with questions about me and Dominic and the Coleraine bomb.' And I told him that was the very reason I had come to see him. And he just opened up to me; it was as if he dearly wanted to tell his story and what he now thought about his involvement in the Coleraine bomb. It was very, very emotional listening to him. He said that they had given a warning, but, through whatever mistake, people were sent up the street by the police to where the bomb was and caught the full impact. He talked about the deaths and the injuries, especially the little kids who were injured. And, you know, he just didn't realise that people would be killed, and deeply regretted that it had ever happened.

Then he talked about his time in Long Kesh and how they kept moving him around because of his efforts to escape. And it was during that time that he met Loyalists and he spoke of some of them in an almost affectionate way, particularly individuals such as Martin Snodden. And it was really that which connected with my own experience as a nurse – that when you were exposed to both sides you began to see the humanity on both sides. And now I was hearing my brother talk in such a positive way about people he would otherwise have been expected to view as enemies. It was at that point that I said to him: 'Sean, if I organise a weekend where you could just meet some of these fellas, would you be prepared to go along?' And he replied: 'Anne, it's the only way forward.'

He told me to contact a woman called Marty Rafferty, for she could tell me where these Loyalists worked. So I met Marty and she drove me up to EPIC, an ex-prisoners' support organisation at the top of the Shankill, and introduced me to Martin Snodden. I told him a bit about my own story and said that I felt it would be good for some of the ex-prisoners to meet up again, and he agreed. Now, obviously it was my first time meeting somebody from the UVF and I was initially uneasy, but I recall how polite and courteous he was – and I think it was his sense of hospitality to me that really was such a good experience for me on that first day on the Shankill. He also introduced me to Allister Lyttle.

Then Marty Rafferty brought me into Andersonstown to see Tony Catney. It was a really mucky old day, and Tony was working outdoors; he was involved along with Paul McKenna and other Republican ex-prisoners on a self-build project. They were building new houses and I was really taken by the fact that they had developed the whole idea for this project while they were still in Long Kesh. I said to Tony that I wanted to bring together some of the fellas that Sean had met inside, basically just to talk.

I went to see others, and none of those invited along refused to come. There was no grand design behind this meeting, I didn't know what I was really doing, I just felt that it would be a positive thing to bring them together and let them chat. Ironically, Sean himself didn't make the actual get-together because he had to attend a funeral of someone who had been close to him.

And as I watched them all sitting talking to one another I had a sense that there was something special happening, I didn't know quite what, but I knew it was something that I wanted to foster, to find some mechanism to allow people like that to meet, just so that they could hear each other's stories.

And as I watched them all sitting talking to one another I had a sense that there was something special happening, I didn't know quite what, but I knew it was something that I wanted to foster, to find some mechanism to allow people like that to meet, just so that they could hear each other's stories.

I should add that I had asked them to bring some of their artwork with them. This was because of my own interest in prison artwork, something that I had become aware of during my brothers' time in prison. When I would go on a visit I could feel their sense of empowerment and excitement when they had something to give you which they had made, whether it was a greetings card or something made out of leather or wood. I also realised that the same thing was happening on the Loyalist side. And I just wondered whether there was some way, when they got out of prison, that they could continue to produce artwork and maybe sell it, create employment. When Dominic had been in Portlaoise prison he introduced me to Brian McGuire, the Head of Prison Art – and who's now Director of the Fine Art College in Dublin – and Brian brought me into the prison and showed me what some of the prisoners were doing. I thought: there's definitely something very important about prison artwork.

So that get-together, and tying in the theme of artwork, was really the beginning of what soon became the Seeds of Hope ex-prisoners project. Its primary focus was to assist the processes of reconciliation and healing through personal story-telling and artistic creativity, and it wasn't restricted to former prisoners.

As part of developing the project I went to see other ex-prisoners and their organisations. Individuals such as Sammy Duddy; I just took a taxi up the Shankill to the UDA offices and Sammy didn't know who I was when I went in to see him. He asked me what my interest in art was and I told him that it was the one thing that was my connection with my brothers when they were inside. They he asked me who my

That was really the beginning of what became the 'Seeds of Hope' project. Its primary focus was to assist the processes of reconciliation and healing through personal story-telling and artistic creativity.

brothers were and of course when I told him it was a bit of shock. Nevertheless, he readily showed me the artwork which they had in the UDA offices. We were actually having an exhibition, in Dublin, of prison artwork and Brian McGuire had asked me if I could get some artwork from the Loyalist community. Brian later went into Long Kesh to do a series of oil-paintings of well-known Loyalists and Republicans.

When I came to realise the openness and basic humanity of those I was meeting on the Shankill I got quite excited. And I thought: if only their counterparts over on the Falls could find some way of meeting them. And that's what the Seeds of Hope project largely became, it was like a network of people. The pattern was that I'd meet somebody and I'd say, 'There's somebody that I know would like to meet you,' and they'd meet, and usually something positive or productive would result from that meeting.

Then, to assist the core group tell their personal stories in a way which would have a wider impact, they sat down and did a Think Tank pamphlet[4], because I had been impressed by the way in which those pamphlets gave the reader such an insight into people's lives. A number of things came out of that pamphlet. For a start it made a positive impact at community level, on both sides – and I

---

4. Island Pamphlet No. 27 *Seeds of Hope: A joint exploration by Republican and Loyalist ex-prisoners.*

think it encouraged people to take this type of story-telling more seriously.

Joanna Berry, whose father died in the Brighton Bomb, which had targeted Mrs Thatcher's cabinet, said on television that she wanted to understand why the IRA did what they did. My brother Paul saw the interview while he was in Magilligan prison, so he wrote to her and a correspondence began. And then when she read the pamphlet, she contacted me and asked me to arrange a meeting with Patrick Magee, who had been convicted of the actual bombing. Sir Harvey Thomas OBE, also injured in the bombing, made a similar request.

At that time we were in contact with different organisations and individuals involved in bringing together victims and perpetrators, primarily to assist reconciliation and healing. Dr. Mark Umbreit from the University of Minnesota contacted me and asked me to arrange for a group of people from here to go over to the US for a series of workshops. Some of those who went later reflected on their experience in another pamphlet.[5] And since then there's been many other people who have been able to go out to Minnesota from other organisations, and it really has broadened their thinking.

There have been other linkages with America. Under the guidance of Professor Paula Garb, Director of the Program in Citizen Peacebuilding at the University of California, Irvine, Seeds of Hope facilitated exchanges of grassroots activists who explored various themes, including gang intervention programmes.[6] Also, with the guidance of Professor John Graham from the Business University, Irvine, and with the enthusiastic support of Dulcie and Larry Kugelman, 22 graduate students travelled to Belfast to study social initiatives on both sides of the communal interface. These exchanges were assisted by community activists in Belfast, among them Joe Camplisson, Jackie Hewitt and Barney McCaughey.

The story of how the name 'Seeds of Hope' originated is fascinating in itself. Many years ago I happened to be in the wilds of Barna, County Galway, with a friend, Barbara. There was some kind of retreat on in this chapel in Barna and she wanted me to go along with her. But it was a lovely Sunday afternoon and I'm sitting there in the chapel getting more and more agitated, wishing I could go

> *I said to Barbara, 'What does that mean?' And she said, 'Seeds of Hope'. I was standing thinking, 'My God, what a lovely name', I was just so bowled over by it.*

for a walk instead. So I left the chapel – with Barbara following behind – and we walked up this wee back road until we came to a derelict bungalow, which obviously hadn't been lived in for many years and was sitting in grounds which were totally overgrown. I went to open the gate and noticed that there was something written on it in Irish. And I said to Barbara, 'What does that mean?'

5. Island Pamphlet No. 53 *A Journey Towards Healing: reflections on a University of Minnesota programme of restorative justice and humanistic mediation*

6. Island Pamphlet No. 34 *Catalysts for Change: a shared exploration by members of Gang Intervention Services (USA), JCDC (Moldova), MICOM (Northern Ireland/Moldova), and Seeds of Hope.*

And she said, 'Seeds of Hope'. I was standing thinking, 'My God, what a lovely name', I was just so bowled over by it. Anyway, we went through the gate and looked through the windows of this old house, the grass up over our knees. Then I had this urge to plant two roses in the garden – I didn't know why, I just wanted to do it, there was something about the place. So Barbara, probably thinking I'm mad, drove me around until we found a nursery which was open, where we purchased two roses. After calling at her house at Salthill to collect a spade we returned to this derelict house and I planted my roses. We then departed the place and I forgot all about it.

However, many years later I found myself back in Barna, and, as the Seeds of Hope project had by then been initiated, I remembered the house where I planted my roses and thought I would look it up again. To my surprise there was now a beautiful bungalow there with a new gate – but still with 'Seeds of Hope' written on it. I knocked on the door and a French girl opened it. I told her the whole story and asked what had become of my roses. The roses were gone, but a small grotto had been erected in that part of the garden. The girl explained that she was part of an international community which had wanted to set up a place in Ireland, and she told me its name – it was the very same one in Paris to which I had brought Sean when he had got out of prison!

[Through the project] we have been able to help establish connections between organisations they might otherwise never have had an opportunity to meet.

The name 'Seeds of Hope' has proven to be very special. And many of the groups we have made contact with over the past nine years, even though they didn't become part of our actual group, seemed keen to take on board the name. And that includes groups of young people in Dublin, ex-prisoner groups down South, and different story-telling groups involving people who have suffered in some way. And some of the ideas we have come up with have been taken forward by other groups. We have also been able to help establish connections between organisations they might otherwise never have had an opportunity to meet.

For example, Seeds of Hope was instrumental in setting up the Forgiveness project – supported by Madison University, Wisconsin – which linked together twelve schools here. The two schools which benefited most were Ligoniel Primary and St Vincent de Paul Primary, because they also subsequently received support from the Program in Citizen Peacebuilding at the University of California, Irvine, which linked them with two schools in LA. This project, entitled 'Picturing Peace', still continues. Hewlett Packard provided the four schools with computers, and the children exchange their 'peace pictures' through the Internet. It was recently launched in Belfast City Hall and the principals were saying to me that the kids just love it. These pictures also involve stories, because the children have to explain why they took each particular picture. And through Seeds of Hope we also got musician Rodney Cordiner and poet Adrian Fox to engage the children in mural-painting and music.

We established links with the Milwaukee festival, in Wisconsin, USA. It involved some 800 kids who hand-painted over 2000 peace flags and made 2000 origami peace cranes with little individual messages of peace. Janet Carr and Nancy Rodgers, who organise the festival, managed to raise $1000 for one of our Seeds of Hope conferences. They also organised a school over there to do an exhibition on the theme of 'Seeds of Hope' and sent us some of the resulting artwork, which we try to include in different exhibitions.

At one stage the Northern Ireland Office wanted to facilitate Seeds of Hope in turning Crumlin Road jail into a self-help enterprise for ex-prisoners. Nothing ever came of it, but I do remember our car journey up to Stormont to discuss the idea. Delwin Williams, a Welsh ex-soldier who lost a leg in an IRA bombing – and who now worked on prison welfare issues from the UDA offices on the Shankill Road and was very supportive of Seeds of Hope – had only got his new prosthetic limb and it was really hurting him. And he was cursing at the lads: 'You fuckers, you're the ones who've left me this way', but in a joking manner. I suppose the nurse part of me was thinking: this is quite something, I know the pain he must be going through, trying to get an artificial limb that suited him, that wouldn't cause him too much pain. Yet he was prepared to sit alongside fellas who would have represented the organisation that had caused him the pain he was going through and he dealt with it not through anger, but with black humour. And I've different memories of how humour has been used in this positive way.

During one Seeds of Hope meeting, discussion turned on the negative use of time and clocks: for example, in the timing of operations, or as timers in bomb-making. And I suggested that maybe they could use the idea of time and clocks in their artwork, but in a positive way, for peace. And not only did they do that, but other groups picked up on it as well, including groups confronting the waste of life – that is, time – by young people who are dependant on drugs.

He was prepared to sit alongside fellas who would have represented the organisation that had caused him the pain he was going through and he dealt with it not through anger, but with black humour.

I was also on the board of management of Prison Arts Foundation and I wanted to do something before Long Kesh closed down. I decided I would ask the OCs of the different paramilitary organisations if they would do something of an artistic nature around this clock idea: whether 'time in prison' or 'time for peace'. So it was arranged for me to go into the Maze and meet with representatives of four organisations – the UDA, the LVF, the INLA and the IRA.

Now, I didn't know who I was going to see that day, I wasn't told. And the first person I was introduced to was Michael Stone. Tom Magill was with me and when we went into Michael's cell he asked me why I was interested in prison art, for I had simply been introduced to him as 'Anne Gallagher'. So I told him why I was so interested, and told him that our house at home was full of artwork done by my brothers while inside. So he asked who my brothers were, and when I told him he was pulling at his long pony tail and said: 'Are you telling me that you are 'Mad Dog' McGlinchey's sister!' I said, 'Michael, I don't like that term. I am Dominic's sister.' And he just stared at me. I said: 'Are you going to throw me out?' He says, 'No, Anne, I'm going to take you on a walkabout.' So he told Tom he wanted some time with me on his own, and he brought me out into the yard. I was with him nearly two hours that day and it was just an amazing encounter listening to his personal story, which is obviously confidential.

And I think that is what Seeds of Hope is – it's something which allows you to tap into those parts of people's lives that others rarely see; almost the sacred parts of their lives.

During our walkabout he showed me a dip in the concrete indicating where the IRA had dug an escape tunnel. I was looking at this dip and thinking of a story Sean had told me, of the time when he had to stay down all night when the tunnel had collapsed. When the other prisoners were being counted back into the cages, one of them had to climb out the window and run back round to be counted twice, to cover for Sean who was trapped in this tunnel. And I'm looking at this dip and wondering whether that was where Sean was trapped, and thinking how ironic it was that it was a Loyalist who was now showing it to me. Then Michael says to me, 'Can you imagine, Anne, if the media got hold of this story – of us talking together.' I said: 'Well, I won't be talking to the media', and he said that he wouldn't be either.

I had to meet him the following Thursday and on that occasion he told me that the media *had* contacted him about my visit but he had only told one of the journalists, because he trusted her. And he said: 'You know, Anne, she asked me what I thought of you, and I told her that you were different from anyone else that came to see me because you didn't come to see Michael Stone the killer, you came to see the artist.'

And to me that was a very profound statement, because he was right. For I never see the killer. Okay, I'd be aware of what individuals have done, but when I'm with them it's their humanity I see, especially when they have enough trust to share some intimate part of their life-story. And I feel that that's what it's all about. When you hear the pain in someone's personal story it helps to transform your image of that person. And I think that is what Seeds of Hope is – it's something which allows you to tap into those parts of people's lives that others rarely see; almost the sacred parts of their lives. Anyway, Michael agreed to do a piece of artwork for Seeds of Hope.

After seeing Michael Stone I was brought over to the LVF unit. At the time it had been recommended that I didn't go there because Billy Wright had been murdered there by the INLA. But I needn't have worried: they were just so hospitable – even though they knew I would be visiting the INLA unit afterwards, the place where Billy Wright's murder had been planned. There were about ten of them, and they showed me their drums and other bits of artwork. They agreed to do a piece of artwork – and it was a lovely piece around the transformation of a butterfly. (On my return visit – to collect the different pieces of artwork – I asked why they had picked that particular theme and they said that because they knew the Seeds of Hope project was all about listening to people's stories, this piece was trying to say that if you pull a caterpillar out of the chrysalis before its time it never becomes a butterfly. And I thought that also was quite profound, because you know, in a way, if a counsellor or anyone rushes someone through their personal story before they are really ready, there can be real damage done.) On that first visit, one of the guys, Gary Blair, brought me down to his cell and said: 'You know Anne, Billy Wright would have really liked to have meet you.' By my return visit Gary had written a lovely poem for me. And then he wrote a letter to Tom Magill and myself saying that the LVF wanted to work with Seeds of Hope. So, I suppose, they sensed some trust in the process of whatever Seeds of Hope represented. And it was something that they wanted to be part of.

I left that unit and was brought over to the INLA unit. I was introduced to Chris McWilliams through the bars of the block. He said that there was no point me coming in because they would be transferred soon to another prison and they didn't have any of their paintbrushes or their artwork. And then I noticed this large painting of Dominic at the entrance to the unit, and I got a wee lump in my throat. So I asked who had done this piece of artwork, because it was very big and colourful, and he replied: 'That's Dominic McGlinchey.' And Tom Magill said to him: 'That's Anne's brother.' McWilliams just stared at me and said: 'Fuck me, you look like him!'

He says, 'Hold on there', and he asked for the unit to be opened up. He introduced me to all the fellas and then said he wanted to talk to me on his own. So he brought me to his cell and I was there for about half an hour, and he talked very openly, although again I can't reveal what he said, but for me it was quite emotional.

For me, art and poetry and music can reveal more of the truth about a person, it's something that you have to dig deep within yourself to find. Not only is it creative, but it can be more honest.

Finally I was brought to meet the IRA group. Later on, Michael Patterson, who ran a class in Long Kesh on fly-tying, arranged for one of them to do a piece containing all these beautiful little flies, based around the theme that although they spent a lot of time making these flies they never got using them for fishing.

Separate from those visits to Long Kesh, the UVF also provided some artwork. And all the pieces were fantastic. For me, art and poetry and music can reveal more of the truth about a person, it's something that you have to dig deep within yourself to find. Not only is it creative, but it can be more honest.

Anyway, when I left the prison that day I just couldn't stop crying. And I was thinking: you meet all these guys, all in their separate little blocks, and even though you know some of their stories and the terrible things they've done to each other and to other people – yet they're so full of humanity, each and every one of them. And somehow you feel that this thing you've tapped into through Seeds of Hope has afforded you access to a different side to them all.

People would often ask me whether I ever felt endangered, or worried that the people I was meeting would be setting me up – because they were bound to be suspicious of someone with my background and mightn't understand why I should want to help them. But I could honestly say 'no', that I had a sense of safety and I had no fear. I certainly never felt any fear when I was on the Shankill. Quite often Alex Calderwood would have walked the length of the Shankill with me, and David Ervine once stood with me while I waited for a taxi, which I thought very courteous of him.

I was never into funding... I felt funding often destroyed the energy of a project, and Seeds of Hope certainly had an energy of its own.

Partly because Seeds of Hope held several high-profile meetings with representatives of both the British and Irish governments, members of our steering committee felt that we needed more structure. Different people – such as Colin Murphy, Director of Glencree – were appointed and paid to help determine such a structure. There were numerous meetings where we discussed the question: just what *is* Seeds of Hope? However, everyone had a different concept as to what it was about and there was never any consensus as to a permanent structure. I am probably the worst offender in that regard, for by nature I'm not a structured person. In many ways, I believe that Seeds of Hope was not so much a project as a *process*, one which facilitated people moving from despair to hope in their own lives.

Furthermore, a primary purpose of these attempts at structuring was to attract funding and I was never into funding. A lot of the energies of many community groups seem to be taken up in filling in application forms, and tweaking them to suit funders' needs, and I could never be bothered with that. I also felt funding often destroyed the energy of a project, and Seeds of Hope certainly had an energy of its own. We did submit different applications to the likes of NICVA and elsewhere, which we felt met all the relevant criteria, but got turned down, so that was quite disheartening and I eventually lost interest in trying.

For me Seeds of Hope was different, because it was never about funding. So for anybody that ever got connected with Seeds of Hope it was totally voluntary. The Community Relations Council gave us money to organise a few conferences, but generally people paid for their own accommodation and food. And there was often some in-kind funding. For example, some people got to go to workshops in Minnesota and other places. And some of the schools here received beautiful books while others got lovely cameras so that the kids could take pictures. But nobody was ever paid to work, so you just had to have a compassion for the work. Indeed, in its nine years of existence, the amount of funding received by Seeds of Hope only totalled £14,000.

Sometimes, I admit, our experience with outside organisations and universities has not always been positive. Academics in particular definitely use people like me. I wouldn't have seen it at the time, but I was eventually to get my eyes opened. Not only do they use individuals, in terms of their time and their contacts, but certain academics have used all the research material they amassed here in order to secure funding for themselves and their own programmes, in America and elsewhere. It has left me very sceptical of such people. I got an e-mail recently from a friend in the US to say that one American academic in particular has made big time out of the research he gathered in Belfast.

Some of the disappointments were more home-grown. I met a German woman in Derry, Rose Prestal, who wanted to do something for Seeds of Hope when she returned to Germany. She ran a candle-making company, and so she made some for us (to this day she still sends over these beautiful three-foot candles, which we give to different community groups). We decided we wanted to give one to both governments as a peace gesture. We also decided to ask the Department of Foreign Affairs in Dublin for a £2000 grant to launch the candle as the logo of Seeds of Hope. At the launch a cross-community group in Derry were going to sing a song especially written for them, called 'Rage against the Darkness'. The Department of Foreign Affairs didn't support us with a grant, but we left the candle with them anyway, telling the minister that if the candle wasn't used in a meaningful way we wanted it back. But next thing, didn't they go ahead with their own candle idea and sent the equivalent of one million Euros worth of 'Millennium candles' throughout the South of Ireland – in small packets that wouldn't fit through people's letter boxes, causing a whole hullabaloo with the postmen. All that tax payers' money wasted, and for what? Yet they turned us down for a small grant, and we weren't just talking about a candle in isolation, we were talking about a whole concept of bringing people together, through both story-telling and art. Sometime later I happened to meet the minister at the Four Courts in Dublin and I said to him how disgusted we were, and then asked him for our candle back. And he said, 'Anne, that candle... my wife burnt it. She loves candles.' He had actually taken it home with him!

However, I must stress that, aside from such disappointments, I have always kept going because of the lovely people I have been able to meet along the way.

32

However, I must stress that, aside from such disappointments, I have always kept going because of the lovely people I have been able to meet along the way.

For example, Rita and John Restorick, whose son Stephen was the last British soldier killed here before the IRA ceasefire. Rita had written me a beautiful letter, a really poignant letter, asking if I could arrange a meeting so that she could give it to the guy who was charged with murdering their son at a border checkpoint. I decided not to pursue her request, I just didn't feel the time was right, but their other son, Mark, asked me to introduce him to some of the fellas who had been involved in the IRA. Which I did, and then he wanted to meet my brother. So I drove him down home and when I told mammy who he was she opened up like a flower to him. I was amazed: I was hearing my mother telling her story *for the first time,* and it was to the brother of the last young soldier killed here. She had never told *us* how she felt during the times the house was raided, having to get up hurriedly, or seeing her sons being taken away – but she was willing to tell Mark.

Somehow when you get an opportunity to really listen to their stories you find out why they've done what they've done, and it gives you a bigger picture, rather than this big rubber stamp of: they're a murderer or this or that, and there's nothing more to them.

Mark said to me, when we were leaving the house, that he'd like to see Dominic's grave. And as I was standing there with Mark, I was thinking of all the sadness I'd experienced at different funerals in that graveyard, and yet somehow Mark was getting an opportunity for healing in his life – by facing ghosts, if you like – because he needed to hear stories that would help him understand the IRA, and why they would want to take his brother's life. We also set out to visit the spot where Stephen was killed, but we got lost and then it got too dark. The Restoricks became very good friends and stayed in our house whenever they came over for Seeds of Hope conferences, and I was invited to Mark's wedding.

So, as I said, somehow through 'Seeds of Hope' you got to meet people who you would normally never get to meet. I've got to meet the most incredible people and experience the tremendous humanity in every one of them. I don't think people are ever born to be bad. And somehow when you get an opportunity to really listen to their stories you find out why they've done what they've done, and it gives you a bigger picture, rather than this big rubber stamp of: they're a murderer or this or that, and there's nothing more to them.

I'll give you another example. I had read in a document how, in the early days in Crumlin Road, Billy McKee for the IRA and Gusty Spence for the UVF had initiated a joint 'no conflict' policy within the prison. So I arranged to meet the two of them, not only to hear their personal stories but with a view to taking them back to where it all happened. And I have a lovely memory of meeting

Gusty Spence and his wife at his house and then travelling in his car to Crumlin Road jail for his first time back there since his release. And then going around the cells with him, and him telling me stories of the people who had been in those cells. And then the prison officer who was there to let us in telling me he remembered the night Dominic had been brought in, and how he had been surprised that Dominic, despite having this fearsome reputation, had been so polite and courteous. And then Billy McKee did the very same thing. It was amazing.

So being able to tap into the vulnerability and that sacred part of people's lives is such a privilege.

To be able to hear people's personal stories is a privilege. Just as I believe it is a privilege to be a nurse. Because when you're working with people who are ill – never mind the Troubles – you're really working at the most vulnerable part of their lives, and it touches you in some way, you just feel that this is a very special place to be. And I'm so glad now to be back full-time at nursing. I work in a respite centre for adults and children with special needs. In particular, I work with young people who present with 'challenging behaviour', and some of them are in wheelchairs and wear mittens and helmets because they self-harm. The only way these kids can verbalise is through hitting out, and quite often I come away physically bruised. So being able to tap into the vulnerability and that sacred part of people's lives is such a privilege.

I think the story of Seeds of Hope is a really positive story for anyone who asks: 'How can you make a difference?' Somehow through Seeds of Hope, even the concept itself, even the name, has been able to make a difference.

Through a programme called 'Cultivating Hope Through Art' I have given numerous talks in universities and prisons throughout the USA – Madison, Wisconsin, Minnesota and California – as well as in Belgium and Sweden. I have also given talks on justice and other issues in different venues across Ireland. I was once asked to speak in the Mansion House, Dublin, on 'learning to forgive'. So I got up and gave my talk and then the next speaker got up. Her only daughter had been murdered by the INLA and after we had made our contributions both of us got a standing ovation. After that we became very good friends and she invited me up to her house and once I stayed overnight. I was in her daughter's room and all her little bits and pieces were still there. And I was lying in that bed thinking that to that women I represented, through my brothers, the organisation that killed her beautiful daughter, and yet she was reaching out to me. I think that's where progress lies, when little seeds like that are planted.

Subsequent to her interview, Anne asked if she could add the following acknowledgements:

First of all, I would like to acknowledge and thank my husband Gerry and five beautiful children – Angie, Cara, Fidelma, Peter and Gerard – who had to put up with me frequently disappearing from our Dublin home to travel to Belfast in pursuit of my vision of peace. Being out of work while convalescing after my car accident, it was Gerry who subsidised many of the expenses I incurred in the course of my efforts. And being so caught up in my Seeds of Hope work I also missed out on getting to spend more time with my three sisters – Helen, Siobhan and Mary. I believe that many grassroots activists who feel driven to follow a vision or a dream quite often leave some woundedness behind among the ones they love.

There have been numerous individuals – ex-prisoners, community activists, professors, teachers and others – who have helped out along the way, in so many different ways. Some I have already mentioned, but many others, because of lack of space, have not been. Among the latter I would include: Michael Appleton, Jeff Barr, Brendan Bradley (sadly no longer with us), Gerry Carolan, Joe Conerie, 'K' Cooke, Joe Costello TD, Jonathan Cummins, Harry Donaghy, Matt Doyle, Bob Enright, Dave Fulton, Janine Geske, Terry Ginley (also no longer with us), Dr Brian Glenville, Victor Griego, Basil Hartey, Claire Hill, Sunny Jacobs, Sammy Johnston, Eddie Kinner, Reg Lacey, Brendan Macken, Ronnie and Anne-Marie McCartney, Liam McCloskey, Bobby McConnell, Frances McDonald, Anne McGovern, Tommy McKearney, Brian McPartland, Liam Maskey, Billy Mitchell, Daphne Myers, Ron Noblet, Irene O'Reilly, Peter Pringle, Nancy Rodgers, Monica Stanley, Hilde Stockman, Dr Maeve Stokes, Michael Tunney, Rosemary Woods, and Mona from Westport who is secretary of Seeds of Hope. Also my cousin Anne, my sister-in-law Marie, and my best friend Bernie, who always had a bed for me when I went to Belfast. I apologise to anyone who I have inadvertently left out of this list.

Lack of space also meant that some community organisations, victims groups and ex-prisoner groups – who either worked closely with Seeds of Hope or provided it with much-appreciated assistance – also had to be left out: among them the Drumcree-Ballyronan Friendship Group, The Clock Project, Ballyshannon Atlantic View Project, Santry PACE ex-prisoners organisation, the Brigidine Sisters Order, Intercomm, Greater Shankill Alternatives, the Live Programme, the Koram Centre, the Tolka Valley Drug Rehabilitation Programme, Survivors of Trauma, and Global Works International Youth Programme.

A final thanks now to the people who have inspired me most to pursue my work for peace: My mother, who really is my hero in life. My family, who gave me their unconditional love and support. And you, Michael, for all the work you do through your Think Tanks: not only is it inspirational but the pamphlets have provided many people who have been hurt during our conflict with a unique opportunity to have their voices heard – and that must surely help in the process of healing and reconciliation.